D0392058

Jenkins, Steve, 1952-202
Animal facts by the numbers :
a book of infographics /
[2022]
33305254352911
ca 11/21/22

FOGRAPHICS

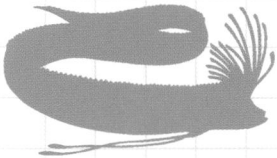

ANIMAL FACTS

BY THE NUMBERS

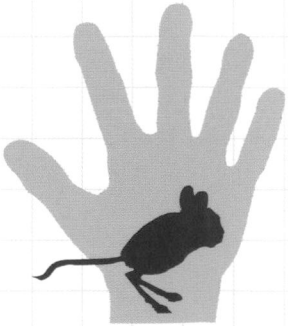

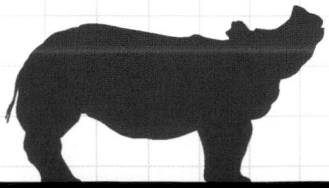

STEVE JENKINS

CLARION BOOKS
AN IMPRINT OF HARPERCOLLINSPUBLISHERS

Contents

5 Introduction

6 One million plus

8 How big?

10 How small?

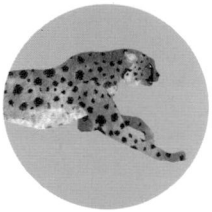

12 Speedy

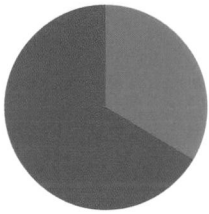

14 Sleepy

16 Fast and slow

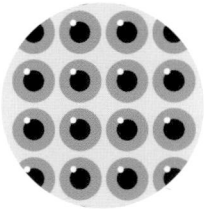

18 How many eyes?

20 Life spans

22 Noisy creatures

24 The deadliest

26 Venomous

27 Poisonous

28 Bite and fight

30 How life begins

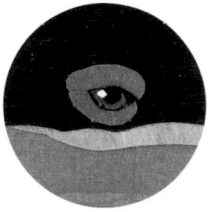

32 Big babies, little babies

34 After the dinosaurs

36 Animals in danger

38/39 Glossary & Bibliography

Animals live almost everywhere on earth. They can be found in scorching deserts and on polar ice caps. They survive on the tallest mountaintops and in the deepest parts of the sea. To exist in these different environments, animals have evolved an impressive range of shapes, sizes, and abilities.

These creatures include a rainforest frog the size of a blueberry and a whale as long as three school buses. There is a fly with a life span of just a few hours and a clam that can live for more than 500 years. And there is a fish that can swim as fast as a cheetah runs and a bat that sleeps for 20 hours a day.

Infographics — charts, graphs, diagrams, and illustrations — present information visually. The infographics in this book can help us appreciate some of the amazing creatures that share our world.

** Words in blue can be found in the glossary on page 38.*

One million plus

Scientists have named about 1,400,000 different animal species. Most of them are insects. There are probably millions more species yet to be discovered.

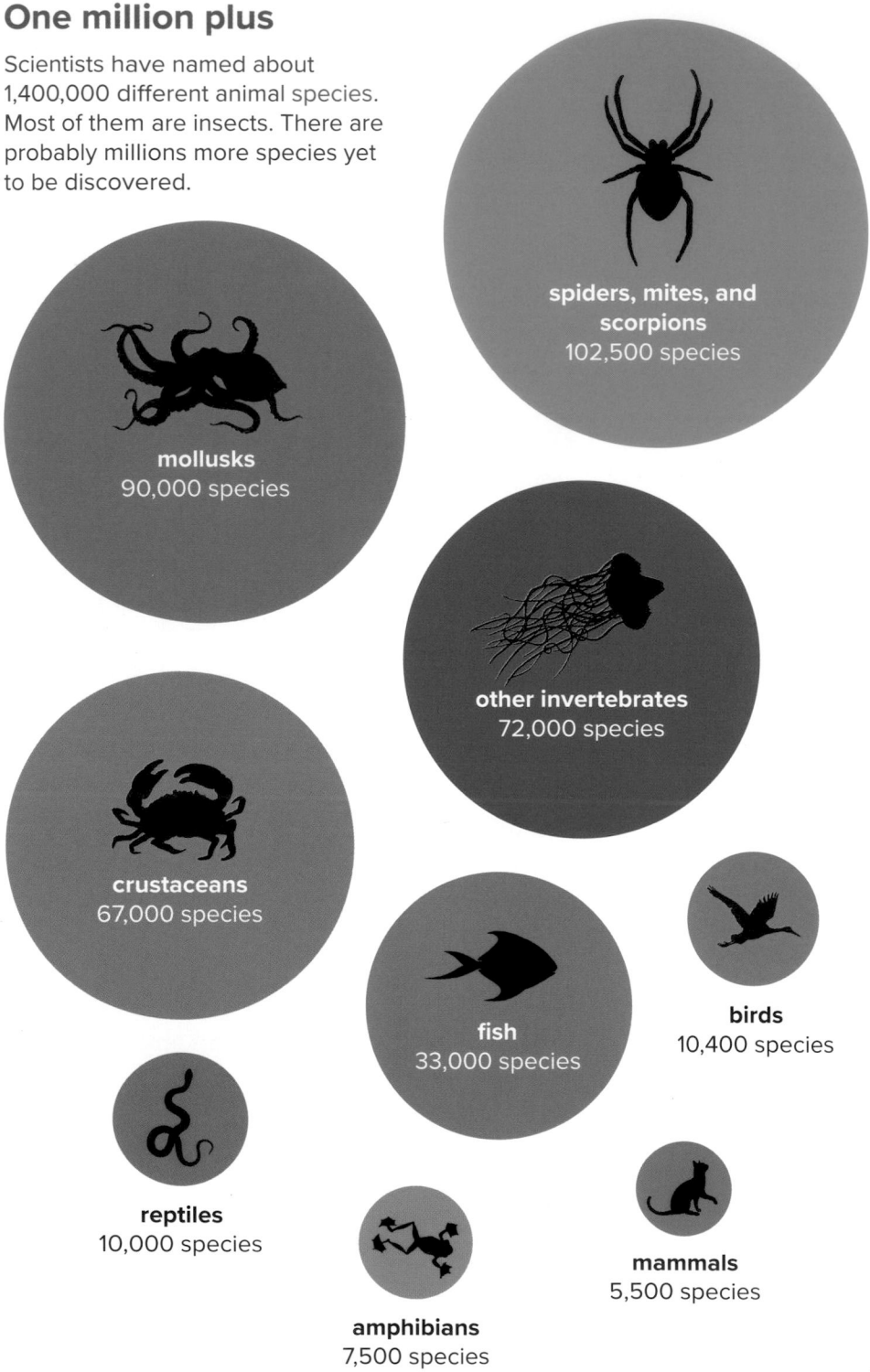

The size of the circles represents the number of named species.

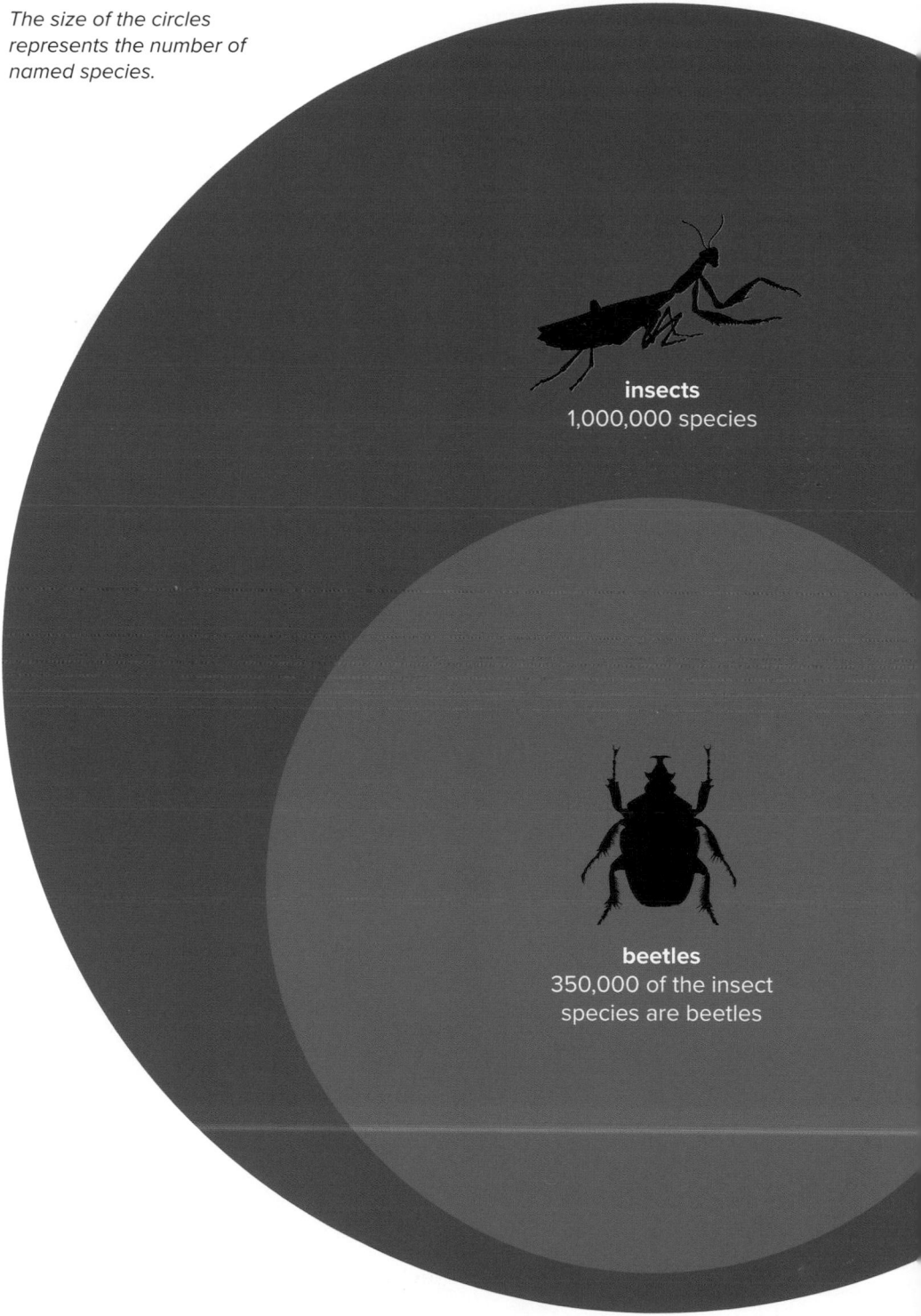

How big?

These animals — some living, some extinct — are shown at the same scale (and compared to an adult human).

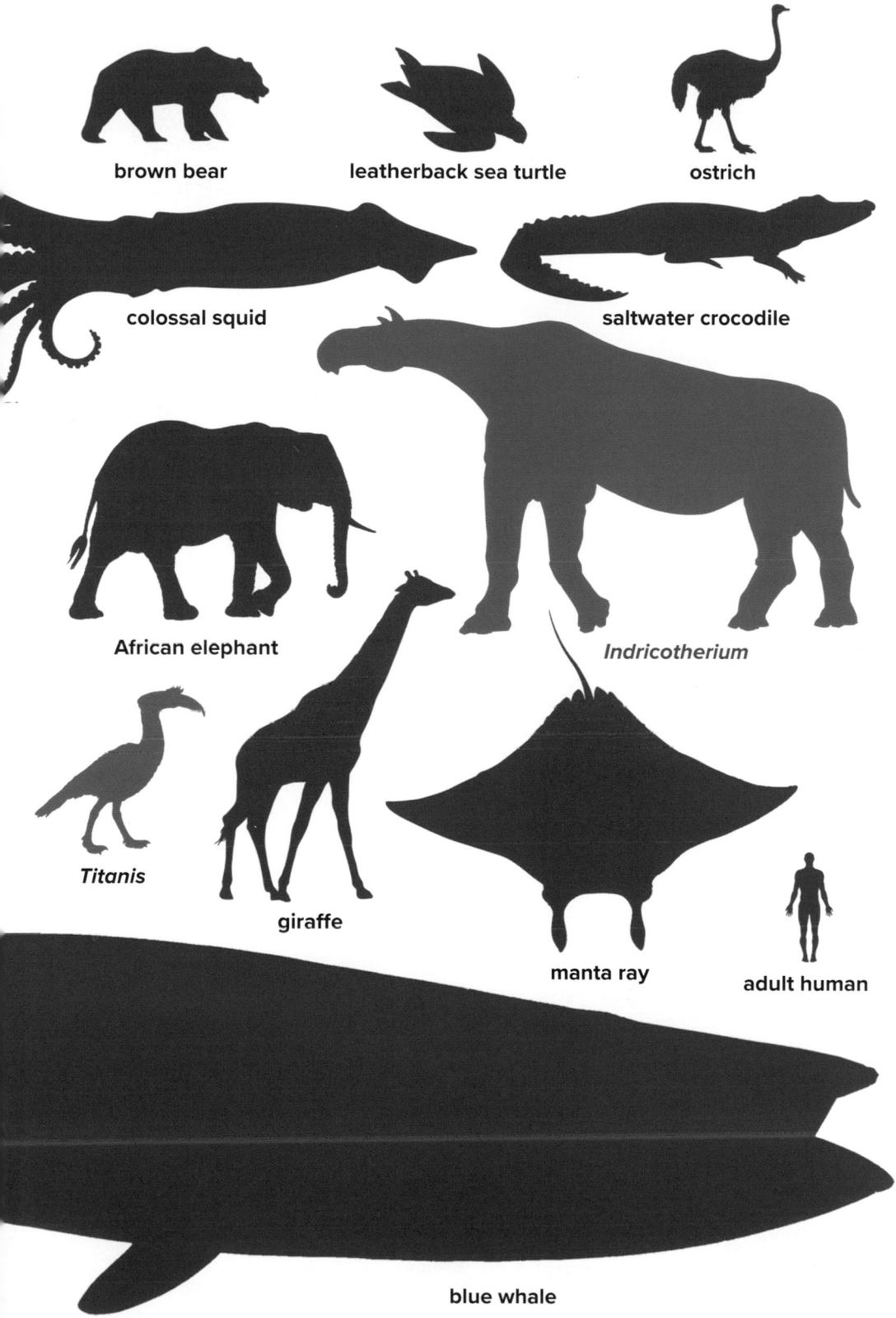
brown bear
leatherback sea turtle
ostrich
colossal squid
saltwater crocodile
African elephant
Indricotherium
Titanis
giraffe
manta ray
adult human
blue whale

How small?

These animals are shown life-size. Many of them are the smallest of their kind.

The **bumblebee bat** is the smallest bat — and the smallest mammal by weight. It weighs less than a Ping-Pong ball.

By weight, the **pygmy shrew** is the world's second-smallest mammal.

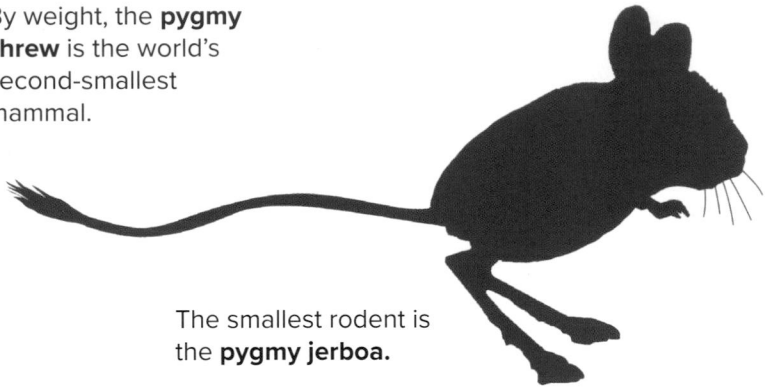

The smallest rodent is the **pygmy jerboa.**

Big and little

The pygmy jerboa compared to the world's largest rodent and an adult human's hand

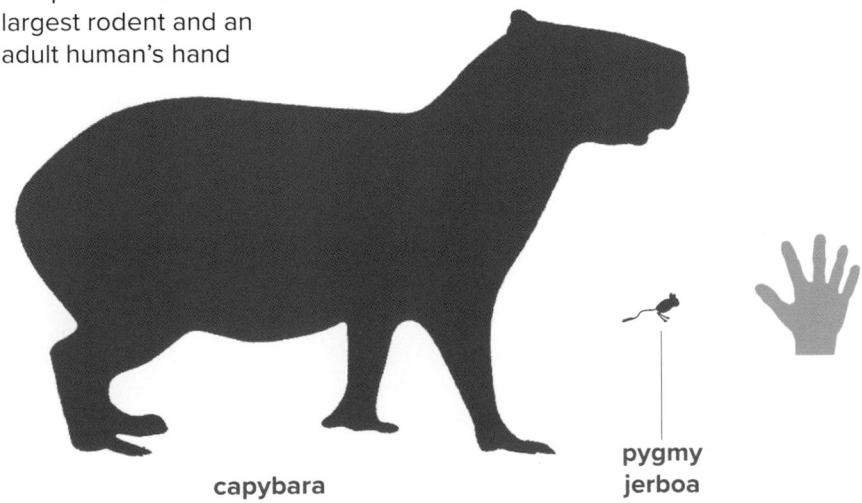

The **bee hummingbird** is the smallest bird. It is not much larger than a bumblebee.

The **slender thread snake** is the smallest known species of snake.

The tiny **Amau frog** was discovered in 2012. By length, it is the world's smallest vertebrate.

A species of dwarf minnow is the world's smallest fish. It was considered the smallest vertebrate until the discovery of the Amau frog.

The smallest known spider is the ***Patu digua***. It is shown above (inside the circle) at actual size, and greatly enlarged, below.

The Amau frog compared to the world's largest frog and an adult human's hand

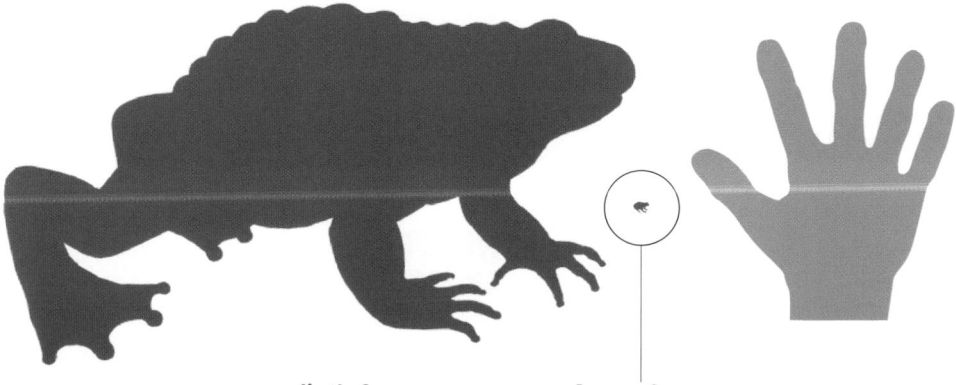

goliath frog **Amau frog**

Speedy

The top speed of some of the fastest flying, running, and swimming animals — and a human

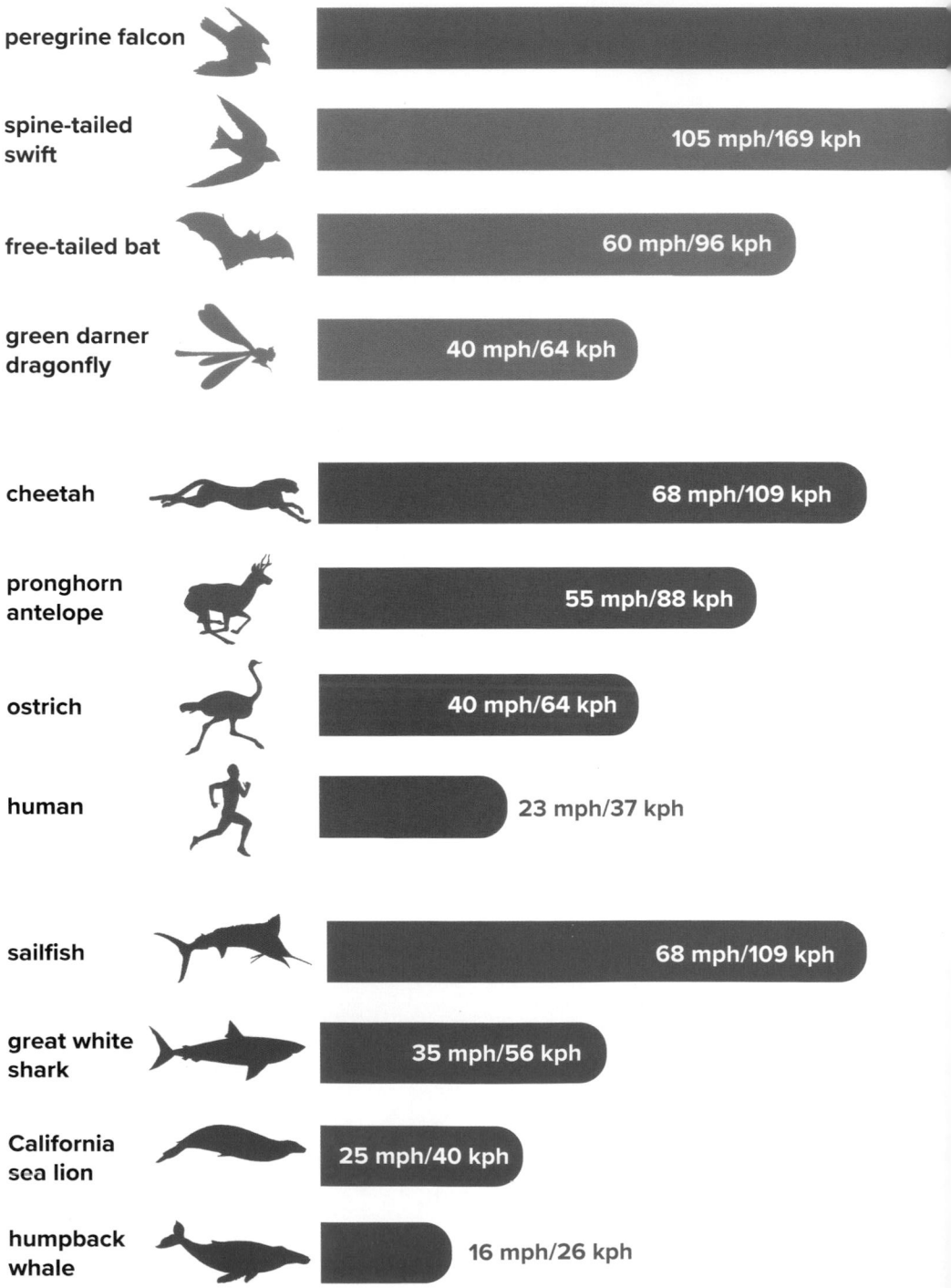

200 mph/322 kph

How many body lengths can an animal run in a second? The champion is a mite that is about the size of a sesame seed. (The fastest human can run slightly more than six body lengths per second.)

The sailfish, the fastest animal in water, is as fast as a cheetah. At top speed, it can swim ten body lengths per second.

Body lengths per second

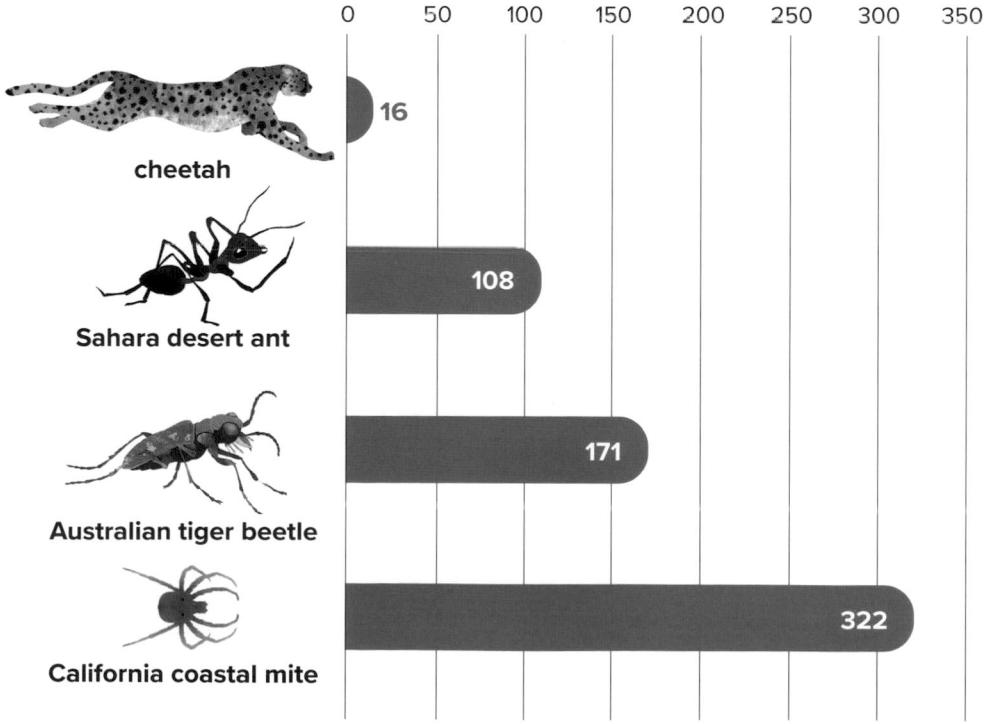

Sleepy

Almost all vertebrates sleep. And it's possible that other animals, such as insects and jellyfish, have periods of rest that are similar to sleep. But the amount of sleep that animals need varies greatly.

The **sloth** sleeps while hanging upside down. The sloth's claws can grip a branch even when it is sound asleep.

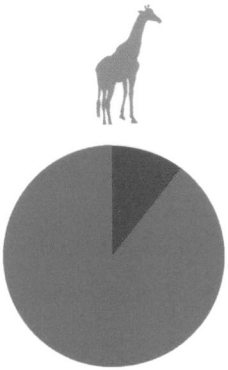

giraffe
2½ hours

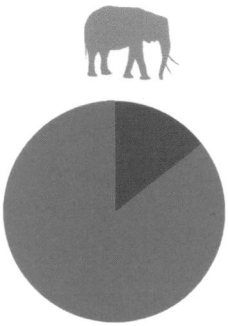

elephant
3½ hours

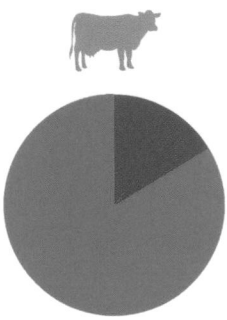

cow
4 hours

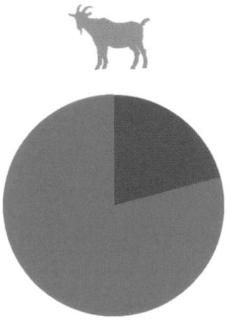

goat
5 hours

cat
14 hours

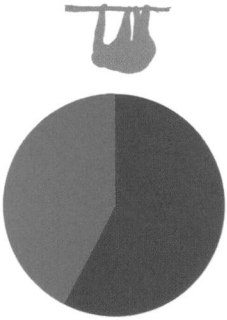

three-toed sloth
14 hours

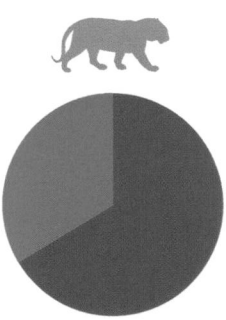

tiger
16 hours

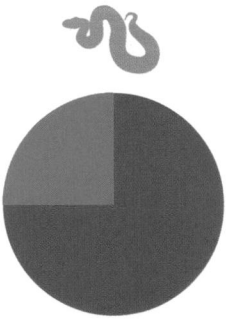

python
18 hours

awake

asleep

By wedging itself in the fork of a tree, a **koala** can sleep without falling.

The **giraffe** needs less sleep than most animals. It sometimes lies down to snooze, but it can also sleep standing up.

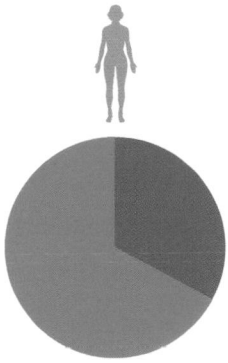

human
8 hours

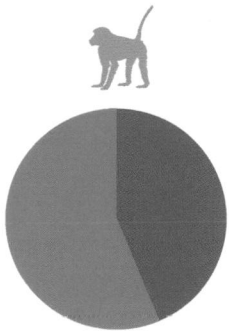

baboon
10 hours

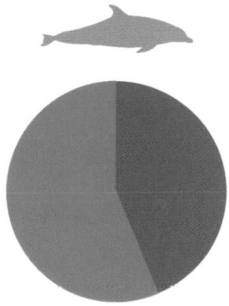

dolphin
10 hours

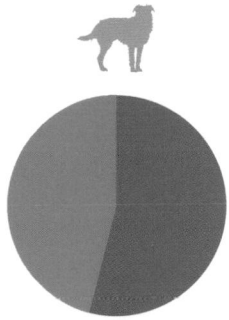

dog
13 hours

opossum
18 hours

giant armadillo
18 hours

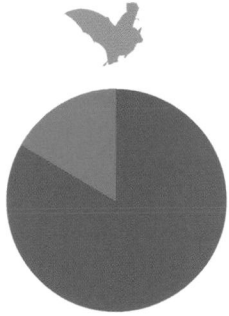

brown bat
20 hours

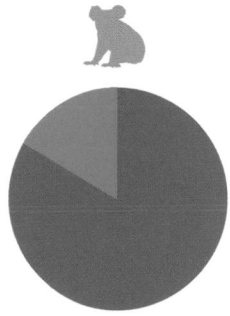

koala
20 hours

The **dolphin** is a mammal, and it breathes air. It sleeps with one half of its brain at a time. The other half stays awake and lets the dolphin know when it's time to surface and take a breath.

Fast and slow

Animal heartbeats vary from rapid whirs to slow thumps. The heart of a small animal beats more rapidly than that of a large creature.

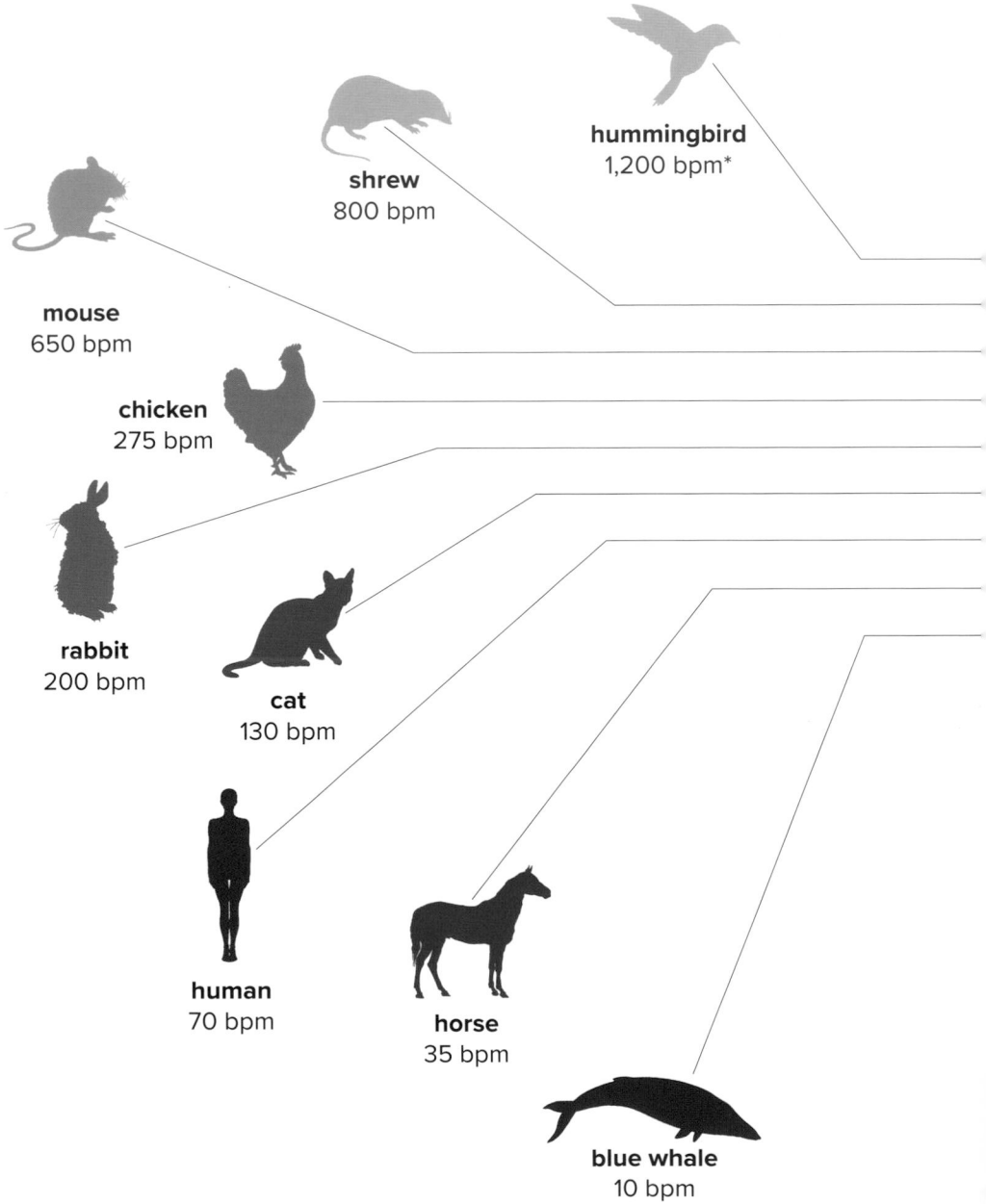

**bpm = beats per minute*

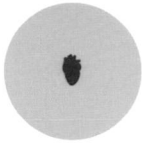

hummingbird heart
(actual size)

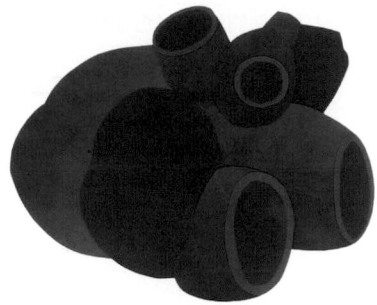

blue whale heart
(compared to an adult
human)

*complete circle = 1,200
beats per minute*

How many eyes?

Humans have two eyes. So do birds, other mammals, and many other creatures. But there are animals with many more eyes — and even an animal with a single eye.

This tiny creature's single eye is a light-sensitive spot, not an eye that can form clear images.

Like almost all vertebrates, this cat has two eyes.

This lizard has a third eye on the top of its head that can detect light.

This fish can look up and down at the same time.

Two of this insect's eyes form images, while three others detect light.

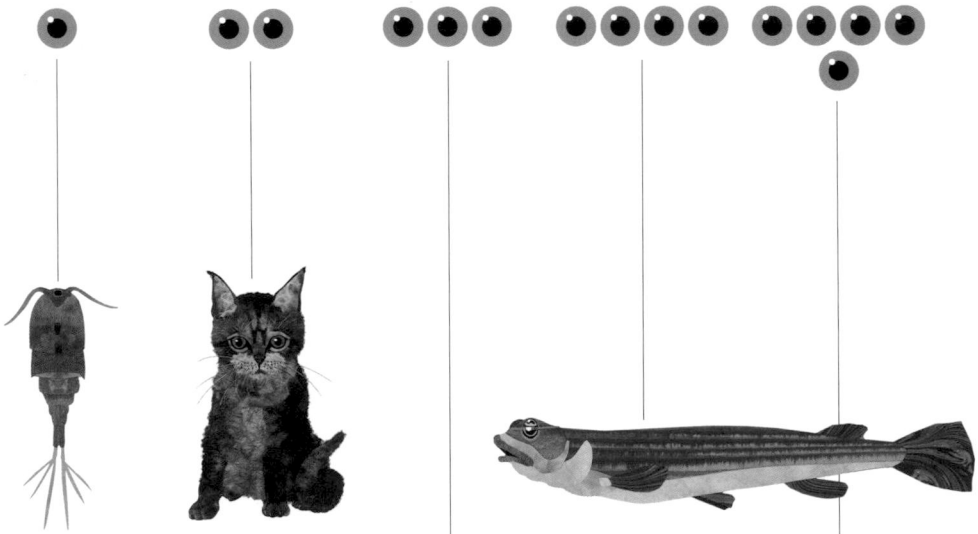

copepod
1 eye

cat
2 eyes

four-eyed fish
4 eyes
(actually four pupils in two eyeballs)

tuatara
3 eyes

praying mantis
5 eyes

A **scallop** can have as many as 200 eyes.

This spider's two big eyes see detail — the other six detect motion.

Two compound eyes form images. The crab's other eyes are light detectors.

In addition to two main eyes, there are five other crude eyes on each side of the scorpion's body.

The **sun star** has a simple eye at the tip of each of its arms.

This jellyfish's 24 eyes are arranged around its bell, or body.

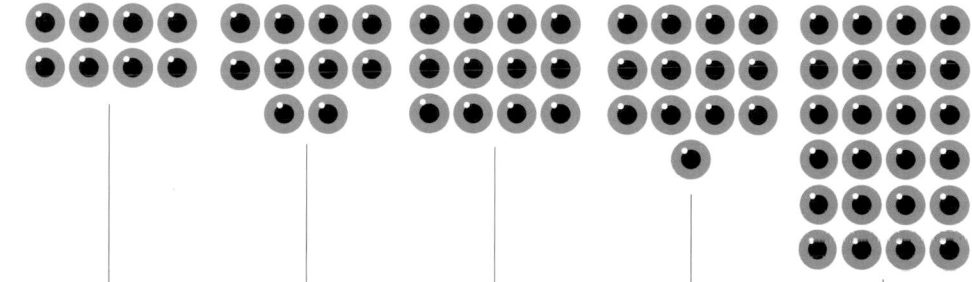

jumping spider
8 eyes

scorpion
12 eyes

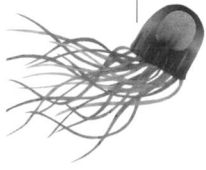

box jellyfish
24 eyes

horseshoe crab
10 eyes

sun star
13 eyes

Life spans

Large animals usually live longer than small animals.

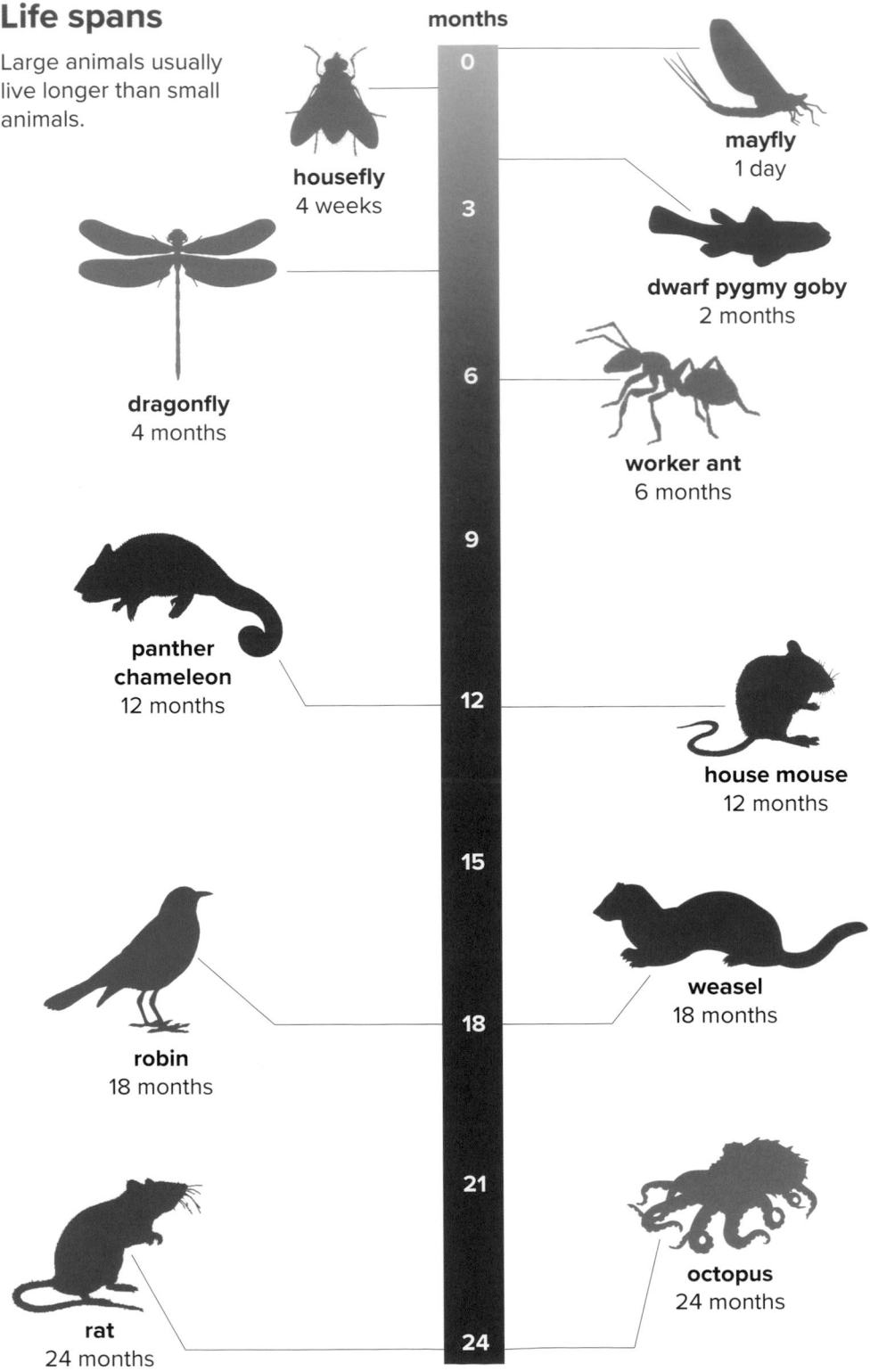

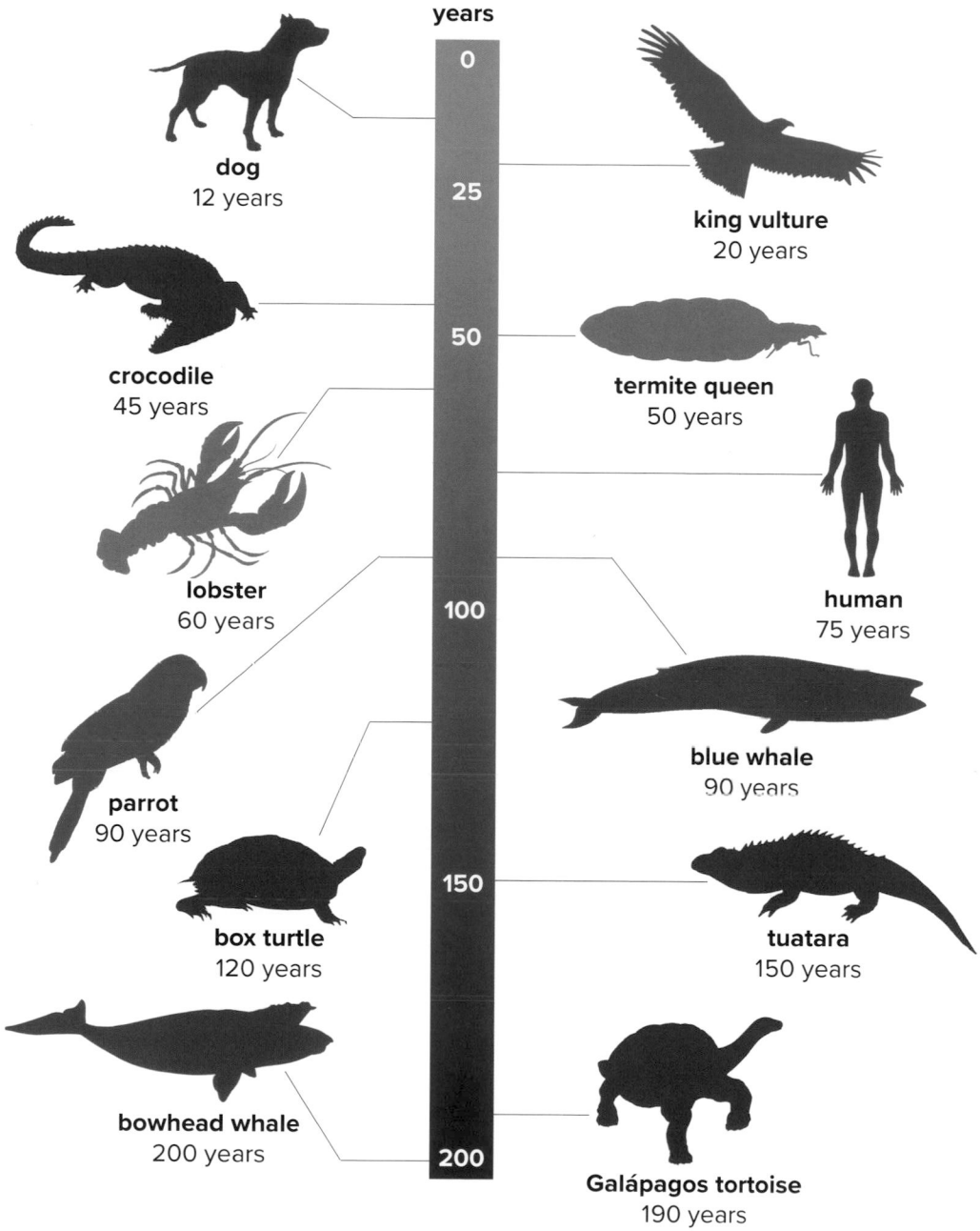

- insects and other invertebrates
- fish
- reptiles
- birds
- mammals

Off the scale

The **quahog clam** can live to be more than 500 years old.

Noisy creatures

Some animals — even very small ones — can make surprisingly loud sounds. They may be signaling a mate, or saying "this is my territory."

By rubbing its legs together, the **bush cricket** makes a sound as loud as a chain saw.

The **coquí frog** gets its name from its ear-shattering call, which sounds like "CO–KEE."

hyena
110 decibels

bush cricket
110 decibels

macaw
105 decibels

alligator
90 decibels

coquí frog
100 decibels

90 DECIBELS **100** **110**

hair dryer

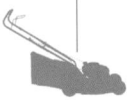

lawn mower

chain saw

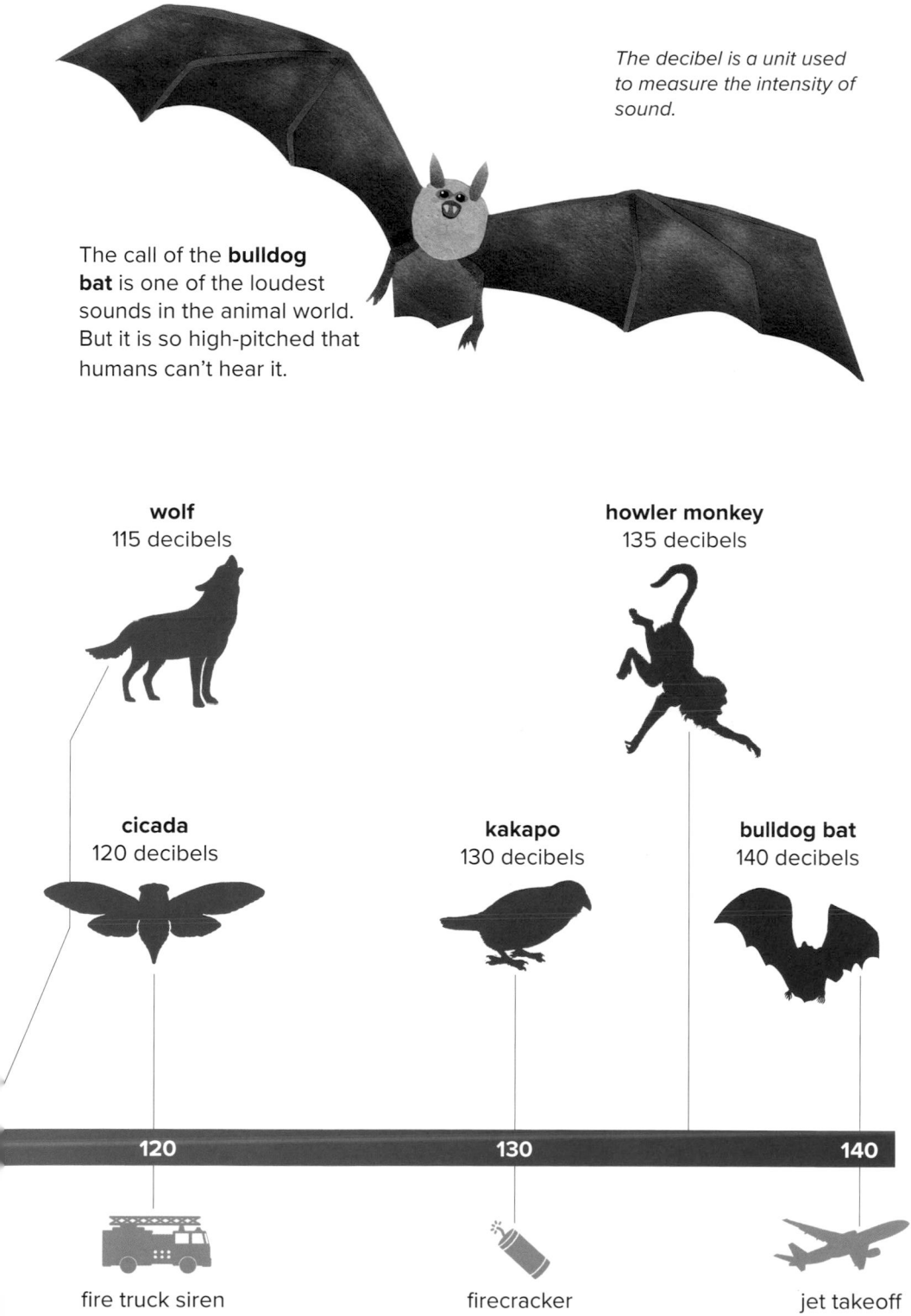
The decibel is a unit used to measure the intensity of sound.
The call of the **bulldog bat** is one of the loudest sounds in the animal world. But it is so high-pitched that humans can't hear it.
wolf
115 decibels
howler monkey
135 decibels
cicada
120 decibels
kakapo
130 decibels
bulldog bat
140 decibels
120
130
140
fire truck siren
firecracker
jet takeoff

The deadliest

The animals that cause the most human deaths are not always the ones that people are most afraid of.

Some 200 people a year die from an allergic reaction after being stung by a **bee**.

About 500 people each year are killed by the fiercely territorial **hippopotamus**.

The **crocodile** is the deadliest large animal. It kills an estimated 1,500 people a year.

Many people are terrified of **sharks**, but they kill only about 10 people a year.

Here are four of the world's most deadly animals:

fat-tailed scorpion
5,000 deaths — venomous sting

= 2,000 deaths per year

tsetse fly
10,000 deaths — carries disease

dog
55,000 deaths — about 500 from injury; most from disease transmitted by bites

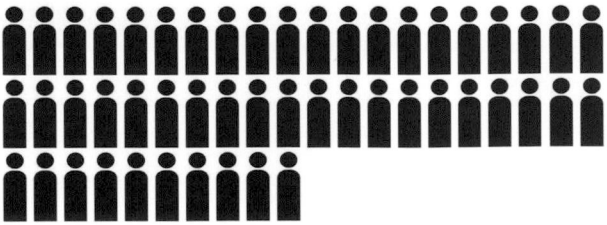

snake
100,000 deaths — venomous bite

The **mosquito** is the deadliest of all. It can transmit several serious diseases, which kill an estimated one million people every year.

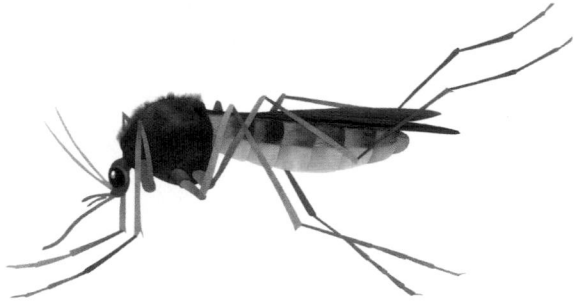

Venomous

Venomous animals inject their toxins with jaws, fangs, spines, stingers, or special stinging cells.

The **platypus** is one of the few venomous mammals. The male platypus has a spur on its back legs that can deliver a painful jab.

funnel-web spider
One of the world's two most venomous spiders (the Brazilian wandering spider is the other)

venom delivery: bite

box jellyfish
The most lethal jellyfish

venom delivery: stinging cells on tentacles

inland taipan
Though this snake is the world's most venomous, it is shy and unaggressive and causes few human deaths.

venom delivery: fangs

fat-tailed scorpion
Its venom is one of the strongest in the animal world.

venom delivery: stinger on tail

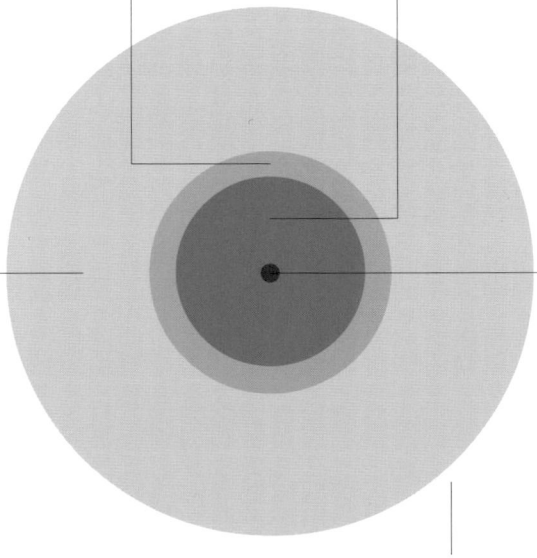

A person stung by a **box jellyfish** can die in as few as three minutes.

The circles represent the amount of toxin that will cause death. The smaller the circle, the more potent the venom or poison.

Poisonous

Poisonous animals have toxins in their skin, fur, feathers, or flesh. They must be touched or eaten for their poison to be dangerous.

The **Asian tiger snake** is the only snake that is both poisonous and venomous. It has poison glands on its neck, and it can also inject venom with its fangs.

puffer fish
This fish is eaten in Japan, where chefs must have a special license to serve it safely.

poison: in the flesh

cane toad
Predators that try to eat this toad often pay for this mistake with their life.

poison: squirts from a pair of glands on its neck

hooded pitohui
This bird gets its poison from the insects it feeds on.

poison: in the feathers and flesh

golden poison dart frog
This little frog has the most potent toxin in the animal world. One little frog contains enough poison to kill ten adult humans.

poison: in the skin

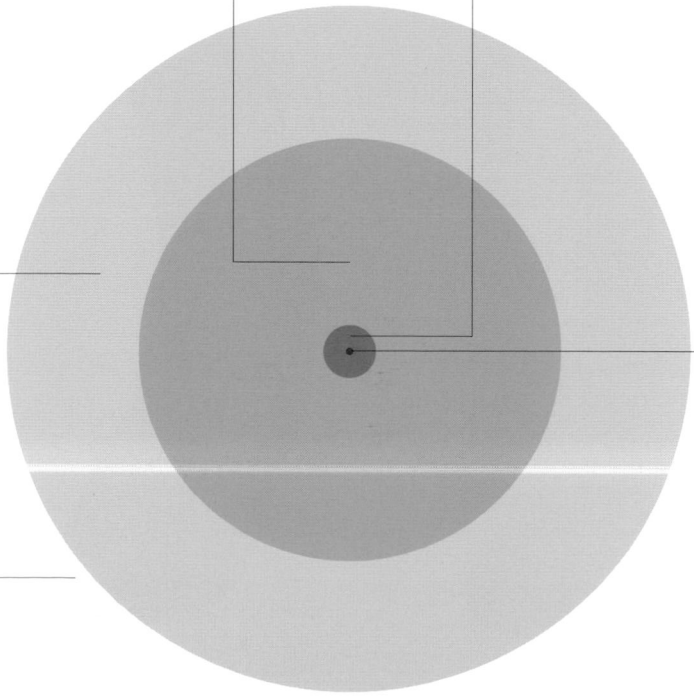

Bite and fight

Animal teeth — including fangs and tusks — come in different shapes and sizes. Animals use them for eating, fighting, injecting venom, and digging up plants.

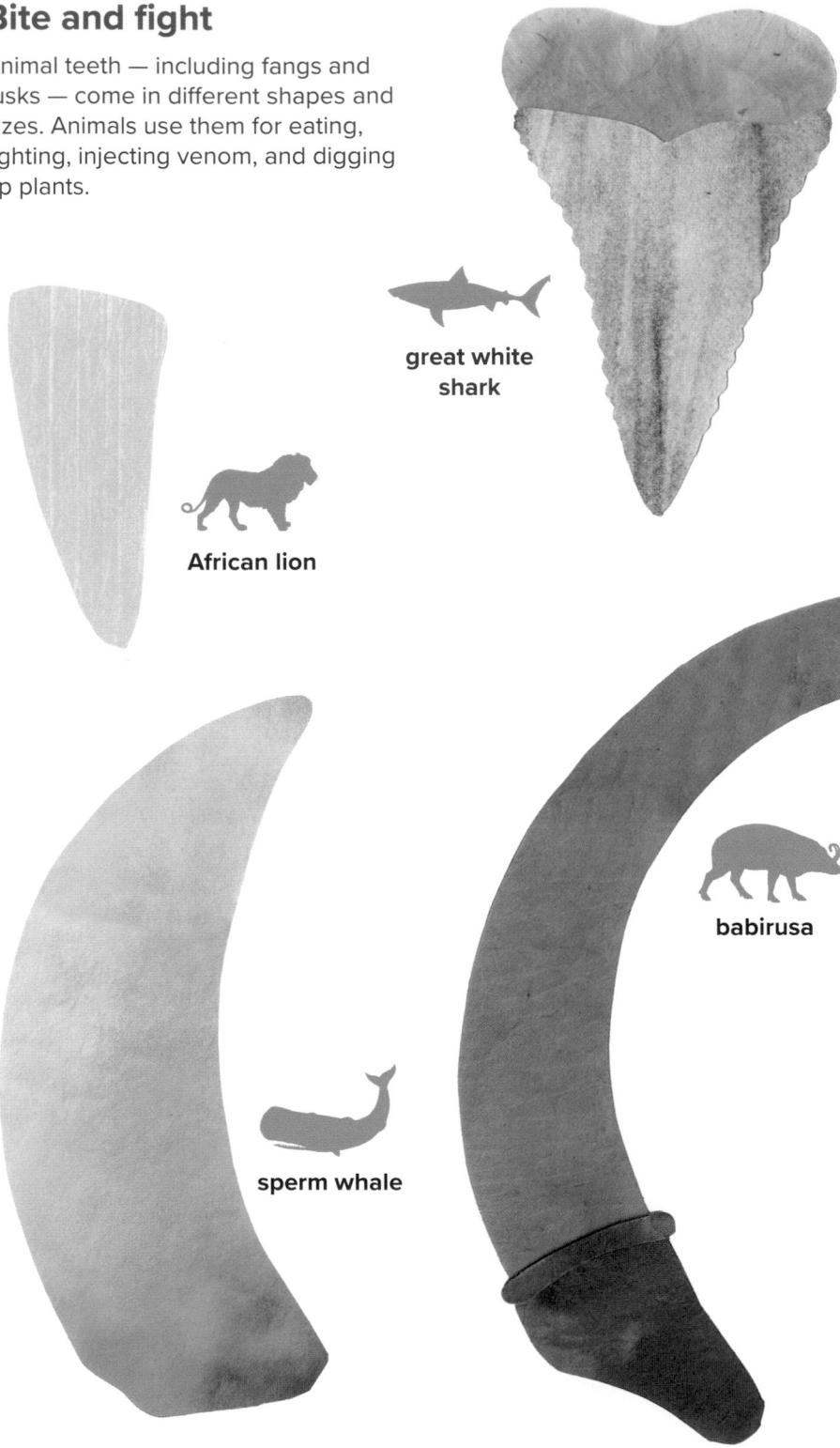

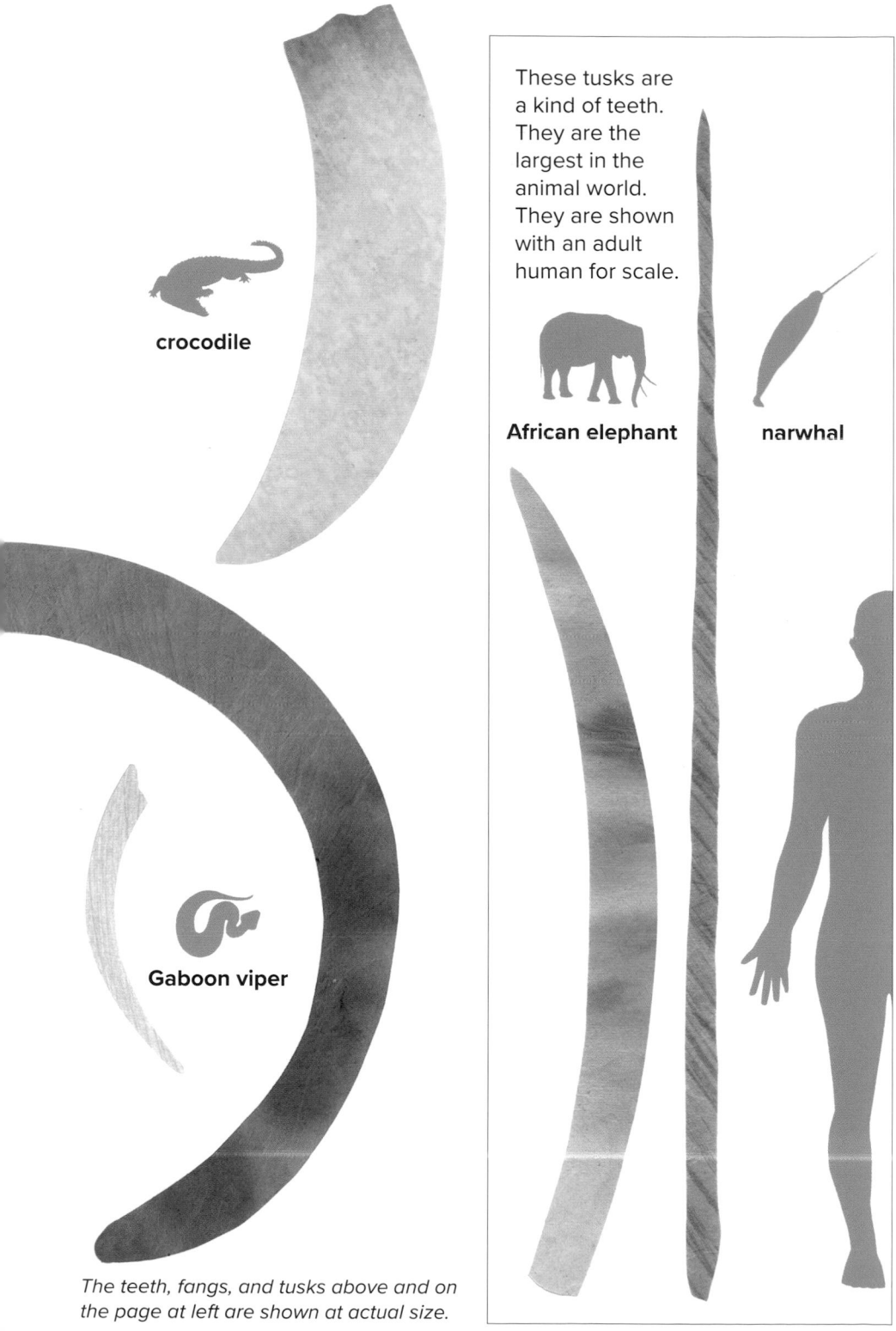

The teeth, fangs, and tusks above and on the page at left are shown at actual size.

How life begins

A few fish, reptiles, and amphibians give birth to live young. And all mammals, except for the echidna and the platypus, have live babies. But most animals lay eggs. Some creatures lay just one egg at a time. Others produce thousands.

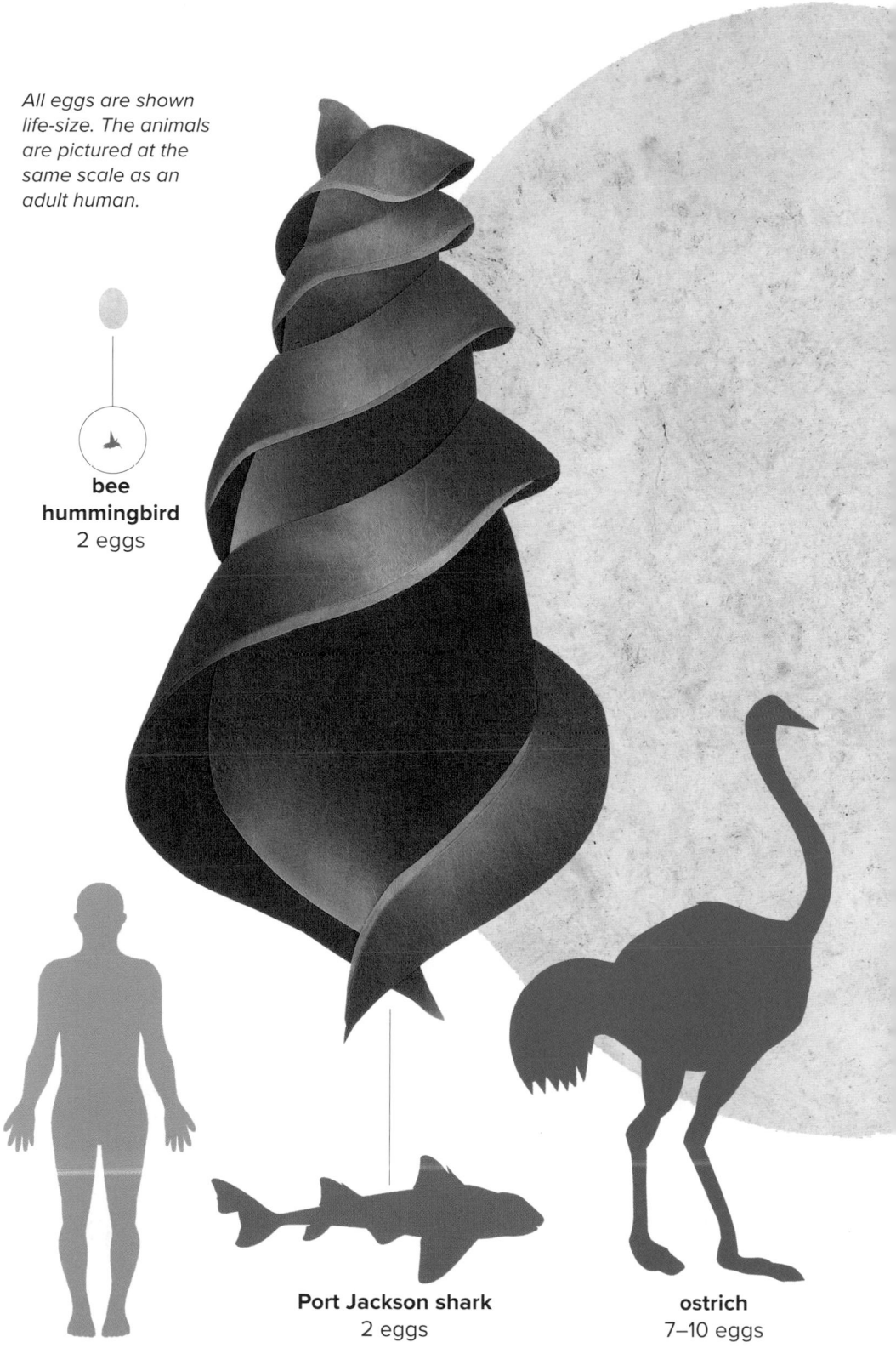
All eggs are shown life-size. The animals are pictured at the same scale as an adult human.
bee hummingbird
2 eggs
Port Jackson shark
2 eggs
ostrich
7–10 eggs

Big babies, little babies

It's not surprising that many large animals give birth to big babies. The biggest of all, a newborn blue whale, can weigh as much as three tons (2,722 kilograms). But other giant animals have small babies.

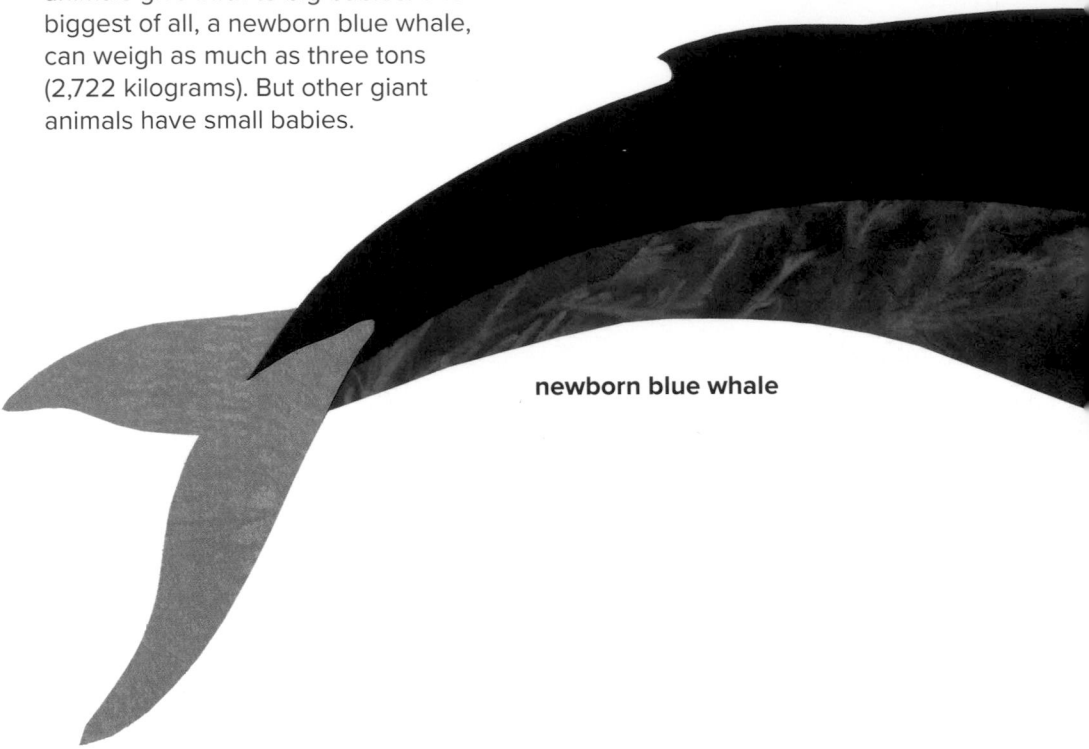

These animal babies are shown at the same scale as an adult human.

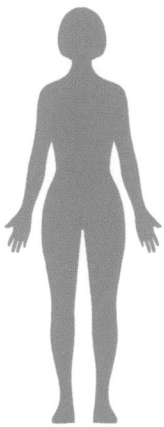

adult human

newborn giraffe

newborn great white shark

newborn elephant

These big creatures — shown below at the same scale as an adult human — produce tiny offspring. Their babies are shown life-size.

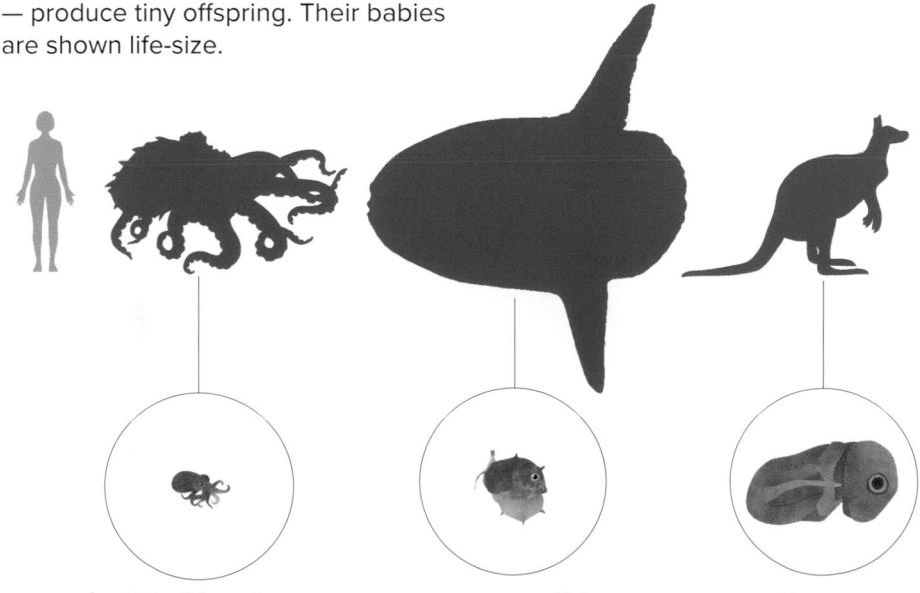

giant Pacific octopus **ocean sunfish** **red kangaroo**

After the dinosaurs

After the dinosaurs died out 66 million years ago, other giant creatures roamed the earth. These animals are all extinct now.

Megalodon was three times as long as a large great white shark (extinct $2^1/_2$ million years ago).

Titanoboa was much larger than any snake alive today (extinct 58 million years ago).

The **giant teratorn** was the largest bird that has ever flown (extinct six million years ago).

This giant **rat** lived in South America (extinct two million years ago).

The animals on this page are all shown at the same scale as this adult human.

Elasmotherium (*e-**las**-mo-**there**-e-um*) was a rhinoceros the size of an elephant (extinct 50,000 years ago).

The **giant ground sloth** was one of the largest land animals of its time. (extinct 12,000 years ago).

Kelenken, a species of terror bird, died out about 15 million years ago.

Daeodon, sometimes called the killer pig, was a fierce predator (extinct 18 million years ago).

Animals in danger

Thousand of animal species around the world are in serious danger. Habitat loss, climate change, hunting, poaching, and overfishing are driving many animals to the edge of extinction.

The estimated number of individuals left in the wild, and where they live

gharial
650
Southeast Asia

North Atlantic right whale
400
Atlantic Ocean

kakapo
200
New Zealand

Assam rabbit
110
Southeast Asia

Amur leopard
80
China, Russia

Javan rhinoceros
60
Indonesia

Lord Howe Island stick insect
24
Lord Howe Island (Australia)

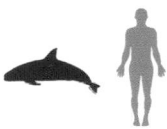

vaquita
10
Gulf of California (Mexico)

harlequin frog
4
Ecuador

Saharan addax
3
North Africa

Yangtze giant softshell turtle
3
China

Glossary

allergic reaction
The body's response to certain foreign substances. Sometimes the body's immune system overreacts, which can be harmful.

climate change
The gradual increase in global temperatures, changes in patterns of precipitation, and sea level rise. These changes are mostly caused by humans burning coal, oil, and other fossil fuels.

compound eyes
Eyes with many individual segments, each of which forms part of an image. They are found in insects and other arthropods.

decibel
A unit used to describe the intensity of sound. A ten decibel increase produces a sound that is ten times more intense.

echidna
Also known as a spiny anteater, the echidna, along with the platypus, is one of the two egg-laying mammals. It lives in Australia.

evolved
Changes in an animal's form or abilities that developed over many generations in response to changes in habitat, climate, or interactions with other animals.

extinct
No longer living. The term is applied to a particular species or group of organisms, not an individual.

habitat loss
The destruction of the places animals live. Habitat can be lost due to natural causes, such as a hurricane or wildfire. Often it's due to human activity such as clearing forests for farms or cities.

Indricotherium
An extinct relative of the modern rhinoceros. It lived about 20 million years ago in Asia, and was the largest mammal to ever live on land. It stood 18 feet (5½ meters) tall and weighed as much as five African elephants.

invertebrates
Animals without a backbone, including insects, worms, jellyfish, and many other creatures.

light-sensitive spot
A patch of light-sensitive cells on an animal that can detect light but not form an image.

poaching
Illegal hunting. Animals may be shot, trapped, or poisoned for food, trophies, or body parts that are sold illegally.

simple eye
An eye with a single lens. More complex than a light-sensitive spot, but not capable of forming images.

species
Members of the same animal species usually look alike, act alike, and can mate and produce offspring.

stinging cells
Specialized cells found in jellyfish, anemones, and other animals. These cells contain a hair-like trigger that fires a venomous barb when touched.

territorial
An animal that defends its territory, usually against others of the same species but sometimes against any animal that it sees as a trespasser.

terror bird
Flightless, meat-eating birds that lived in the Americas from 60 million to about 2 million years ago. They were fast runners with big, sharp beaks. *Kelenken,* the largest of these birds, was one of the top predators of its time.

toxin
A poison or venom produced by a living organism.

vertebrate
An animal with a backbone. Fish, reptiles, amphibians, birds, and mammals are all vertebrates.

Bibliography

Amazing Animals Q&A. By David Burnie. DK Publishing, 2007.

Amazing Numbers in Biology. By Rainer Flindt. Springer, 1996.

The Animal Book. By Steve Jenkins. Houghton Mifflin Harcourt, 2013.

Animal Fact File. By Dr. Tony Hare. Checkmark Books, 1999.

Animal Records. By Mark Carwardine. Sterling, 2008.

Egg: Nature's Perfect Package. By Steve Jenkins and Robin Page. Houghton Mifflin Harcourt, 2015.

The Encyclopedia of Animals. Edited by Dr. Per Christiansen. Amber Books, 2006.

Life. By Martha Holmes and Michael Gunton. University of California Press, 2010.

The Life of Mammals. By David Attenborough. Princeton University Press, 2002.

Nature's Predators. By Michael Bright, Robin Kerrod, and Barbara Taylor. Hermes House, 2002.

Sleep and Rest in Animals. By Corine Lacrampe. Firefly Books, 2003.

Venom, Poison, and Electricity. By Kimberley Jane Pryor. Marshall Cavendish, 2010.

Weird, Wild, Amazing! By Tim Flannery. Norton Young Readers, 2019.

Wildlife Factfinder. By Martin Walters. Dempsey Parr, 1999.

The World of Animals. By Desmond Morris. Jonathan Cape, 1993.

For Henry

Clarion Books is an imprint of HarperCollins Publishers.

Animal Facts by the Numbers
Copyright © 2022 by Steve Jenkins
All rights reserved. No part of this book may be used or reproduced in any manner whatsoever without written permission except in the case of brief quotations embodied in critical articles and reviews. For information address HarperCollins Children's Books, a division of HarperCollins Publishers, 195 Broadway, New York, NY 10007.
clarionbooks.com

ISBN: 978-0-358-47012-0 hardcover
ISBN: 978-0-358-47013-7 paperback

The illustrations are cut- and torn-paper collage.
The infographics are cut-paper silhouettes and the graphics are created digitally.
The text type was set in Proxima Nova.
The display type was set in Berthold Akzidenz Grotesk.

Manufactured in Italy
ROTO 10 9 8 7 6 5 4 3 2 1
4500846446

First Edition